The Pull

156 Poems Inspired by Tarot

Brianna Christine

Written, edited, and designed by Brianna Christine

ISBN (Paperback) 979-8-9944920-0-0
ISBN (eBook) 979-8-9944920-1-7
Library of Congress Control Number 2026900396
Published by TCS Legacy, Cleveland, OH

This is a collection of whispers and thoughts exploring the cost of being through tarot. As such, some content may feel heavy.

It is.

Let's share the weight.

Close your eyes
you can see
more clearly

follow my lead

(or don't)

The Fool (upright)

I never
told you
it was
happy
ever
after

Is it really
my fault

I promised
adventure
and that's
what you got

The Fool (Reversed)

If I could
I would put
myself on repeat
the one I know is me

not the one that
you’ve met

I am a bridge that
isn't seen

my respect is granted
your awe is guaranteed

it's been
more
than earned

The Magician (upright)

Have you ever forgotten how to

speak

I know the words
but the
breath

it's
too
heavy in my lungs

The Magician (Reversed)

It's not your head
or your heart
it's

it's what happens when
you smell fresh pretzels
or bite into a crisp apple

it's a sip of water
in the middle of the night

it's something you
can only appreciate
if you don't think
too much about
the process

The High Priestess (upright)

It's easy just
Obviously you need

What do you mean a stomach ache?

Just
Have you tried doing
Maybe just

What is there to be nervous about?

It's easy just

Can you hear me?

I said

And then

The High Priestess (Reversed)

If you don't want to be
nurtured

that is fine by me

I have an inner child
waiting
desperately

The Empress (upright)

I wonder if you
would have been
nicer
if you knew I would

survive
this long

The Empress (Reversed)

I answer to
who?

You cannot knock me
from the
throne
I built

you
couldn't even reach
the seat

The Emperor (upright)

I will
watch as
your memory
chokes on the
thought of
my success

The Emperor (Reversed)

Study the rules
So you know
Which to keep
Walk through the dark
While the rest
Stay asleep
The road might feel rigid
But that's how they play
Your virtue is bright
Let that lead your way
Find meaning within

And comfort with out

The Hierophant (upright)

Have you ever
wondered how
many heads an
idea
has traveled through
before it
got
to yours

I have seen and
released
so many

The Hierophant (Reversed)

Perfectly lined bricks
pave the way for
exquisite woodwork
on the door
short cozy halls
a fireplace in the living room
pictures lining the walls

what it looks like
doesn't really matter

I see just what I need
beautifully balanced and steady
like drinking coffee
with your weed

The Lovers (upright)

Listen to the
birds
watch the
color
leave his face
have you ever
enjoyed
the metal in
blood

I long for the
taste

The Lovers (Reversed)

I feel like a
turtle
who has made
his way
finally
across the highway

and into
the river

The Chariot (upright)

If I timed it
just right
do I still
take
the blame
it was
arguably
simply

coincidence

The Chariot (Reversed)

There is no such
place as the
end

I wish they knew
what the roar truly means
so they would
yell too

but for now we
find enough with
each other

Strength (upright)

I thought if
I kept going
well I knew I might
crack but I
thought if I kept
going

I should have stopped sooner
I just thought if I
could just keep going

it was right there I
dropped it all

should have just stopped
sooner but I just thought that if

I could keep going
maybe

I'd be worth it

Strength (Reversed)

I'm not scared
to be alone anymore
I saw the girl that
lives in the walls

we both tried to hide

she was so bright
I couldn't look away
we talked for hours
without saying a word
I wish I could thank her

it feels weird as hell
to think I owe
everything
to my 5 year old self

The Hermit (upright)

She just likes to
be alone
or so she says
I often wonder
as I look at her

she doesn't let
me often

if I'm lucky

she looks in the
mirror and tells me
she wishes
she loved me

The Hermit (Reversed)

The longer you spend
in your reflection
and loving what you see
you will understand

your eyes and nose
those who came before

I am not my ancestors
wildest dreams
nor more than
what I reached for

I am
exactly
the one we

screamed for

The Wheel of Fortune (Upright)

I wonder if
turning harder
might work

spinning but
why won't anything
move
I can't
find any way

I'm stuck

please

there's not enough
room

The Wheel of Fortune (Reversed)

Now

I wish I could see
through your eyes

To be completely
impartial

What a relief
I had
settled on
numb

Justice (Upright)

I see
why they say
lady justice
must be
blind

I should stop being
surprised

when she can't see
me

Justice (Reversed)

If you are quiet
the wind will speak

stop running
the breeze is
fast enough

The Hanged Man (upright)

I have
already offered to
help you
come down

if you want to stay
here
I can for a bit too

at least
until you realize
how close the
ground is

The Hanged Man (Reversed)

Just as the
soil must
be tilled

Sorry it
hurts did you
think it would

feel good

to shed all
you knew

Death (Upright)

Fresh blueberries in October

late blooming flowers

the first warm day after
frost has already hit

I deny any rebuttal

There is
absolutely
nothing

I'd rather be doing

Death (Reversed)

I hope some day
to find comfort in
the breeze as it passes

instead of wishing
to be a
leaf

Temperance (upright)

I am certain I
I can control
myself

just a little
more

yes, a little more sounds
fine

I’m sure I shouldn’t
but I would like
just
a little

I'm fine I'm in
control
of myself
I would just
like a little
more

Temperance (Reversed)

I take more than
I am willing
to give

I want
to consume
a bit of everything

it won't hurt if it's just
a
little

The Devil (upright)

Have you
tasted what it feels like
to not be afraid
of the shadows

I spoke with
the things
living there
they were only trying
like me

the reward is
they now rock
me to sleep

The Devil (Reversed)

You don’t have to be
standing
just breathing

don't leave
before the fog
clears

you can take
your time

you can also have
some of
mine

The Tower (upright)

How could I
tell we were
on fire

I smelled the
smoke
but it was
there when
we started

The Tower (Reversed)

Do you know
what happens
when something
gets compressed
so much it can't
do anything but
explode

You are dust
be in the wind
get in their eyes
make their
mouths water

The Star (upright)

You have always shone
this bright

make a wish on
yourself

The Star (Reversed)

Do you hear
your thoughts

No, your thoughts

No, your thoughts

No, your thoughts

make sure they are yours
before you listen

The Moon (upright)

What if they're right
what if they're right
what if they're right

What if I'm right

A new
stronger
prescription for glasses
after pretending
squinting
works just fine

The Moon (Reversed)

I am certain this
is the way
life is meant to
be felt

under my glow
they have bloomed so
beautifully

I am certain this
is what I am made for

I am dreaming
eyes wide open

failure
fears my presence

I have never dimmed I
only found a different
spot to shine

The Sun (upright)

How can I
keep
trying

they claim to be
impressed
I just keep
raising the bar
for myself and then
I wonder why it's
out of my reach

The Sun (Reversed)

It would be a lie
to say there are
no regrets

but to say I am glad for
the mistakes is also
not true

I have found comfort in
the contradiction

Judgement (upright)

I watch the
future come and go

the comfort in
familiarity

rocks in my pocket

I'm not sure

I want

to float

Judgement (Reversed)

Such a lucky thing
to be able to say
I saw the light I
always knew was
there
I
wish I knew sooner
I didn't have to
go so far
to find
wholeness

I am whole
I am
ready to do
more

The World (upright)

It's funny they
say
I'm
too hard on myself
they say
I've done so well

I'm a sweater
with a
loose string and
I'm just gonna
pull

maybe I'll be
worth my weight
in wool

The World (Reversed)

Out with the old
in with the new

the salt in the seas
the salt in me too

everything is in my favor now

I'll fill these cups
that is
my vow

Ace of Cups (upright)

Maybe if I
tread lighter
the waves will
push me forward

I'm not drowning

yet

Ace of Cups (Reversed)

The world
will never
run out of
love

I have found the spring
where compassion flows

it told me
there is no end

Two of Cups (upright)

If an end
can
make a new
beginning
I wonder if in
this next
one

I can understand
give
and
take

Two of Cups (Reversed)

I'm glad to have
want
woven deep with the
need

we've accomplished so much
thank you for staying

with me

to see

Three of Cups (Upright)

If you don't mind
nothing to see here

the party is over

if you don't mind
it's time for you to go now

I wish I could go

but I live
here

Three of Cups (Reversed)

I recognize the
luxury
of time and
space
to just sit
and
to think

the luxury of
rotting in my own
brain

Four of Cups (Upright)

Beginning to remember
when they prayed

even if I don't believe

something heard

maybe just me
and that seems like

enough

Four of Cups (Reversed)

Why won't you
try
the water only
feels

deep
because you are
face down
if you stand
up
we can walk

together

I will only
wait
so long

Five of Cups (Upright)

They say if
you're trying to save
someone drowning

they might accidentally
pull you down

I'm not sure it is
always
an accident

I think
she'd like to have used
my head as
a buoy

Five of Cups (Reversed)

I was thinking
of you while
kneading my dough

I saw a
home where
tension doesn't
leave a bitter taste on
everything in it

I am glad it is
mine

Six of Cups (Upright)

It's my own fault
I am
angry at the rock for
not blowing in the wind

what is
mixed with
what
could be

Six of Cups (Reversed)

I thought it was
hopscotch

why are we
jumping over each
other

you all look
like me

why am I
so many

Seven of Cups (upright)

If my thoughts are
reality and
reality is my thoughts
I will just think
I am the exception
to any rule

for extra precaution
I will pretend there
is nothing that scares me

your reality is a
suggestion

Seven of Cups (Reversed)

I know
you think
I think
I know
it all

I'd rather walk
barefoot

on sharp rocks
and broken glass
than to stay here with you
to rot in these walls

Eight of Cups (upright)

I know the hole is
only growing with
each heave of the
shovel but if I
stop then I am
worried I may have
wasted my time

looking down so
I can't really tell how
deep it's
getting

if this is
the wrong way
I'd probably

see a sign

Eight of Cups (Reversed)

You can call it
luck
if you like

I don't mind

I am flattered
you don't
notice the
scars

Nine of Cups (Upright)

They keep asking
how I’m feeling
as if I should have
a clue

seems we all have
settled on

I'm good thanks
How are you

Why bother even asking
anyone
besides
myself

Nine of Cups (Reversed)

I have found
myself
in the stars

there is more
than enough
space
for
you

Ten of Cups (upright)

Sure
you have only
been wrong while
trying to see their virtue

that doesn't always
mean someone
is trying to
hurt you

Ten of Cups (Reversed)

Excited to see what
is around the corner
the memory of being
afraid is surely not mine
I'm
excited to find what
is ripe and sweet
the idea of not knowing
is a plastic bag
on my head
I'm
excited to smell something
new and
overwhelming
there is nowhere I won't
look
I'm excited
to feel anything

different

Page of Cups (upright)

If wanting isn't enough
and thinking means nothing

If we're all just playing dress up
and phones are always buzzing

I'll just
light the fireplace
on the tv

Page of Cups (Reversed)

I often wonder how
she
keeps me wanting more
her
heart is so pure I wonder if
she
would notice if
I
followed close behind
she doesn't look back
I'm enchanted by
her
shine

Knight of Cups (Upright)

An almost comical cliche
with my head in a ditch

I would be less concerned
if as women we loved

not in competition

and
if as men we could talk
and

be willing to listen

Knight of Cups (Reversed)

I have so
much more than
enough I am happy to
share

it doesn't matter to me
if you think you
tricked me
I don't consider love a
waste of
time

Queen of Cups (upright)

The earth fooled her
warm
cozy
2 eggs beneath

she doesn't know
she was spared
a full clutch

watching snow, unconcerned
she's supposed to be
here
always
happy as ever

her eggs will never hatch
but even if they
did

what next

Queen of Cups (Reversed)

You are a salmon
swimming upstream

I'm the bear that
could catch you

Be glad you are
small

and I
am not
hungry

King of Cups (upright)

Even if your limit
is equal to the depth of
the ocean

even if your love knows
no bounds

the sun sets on every bow
eventually
but
it will rise again tomorrow

King of Cups (Reversed)

I have lit the candles
I have lifted the floor

I know
what I'm doing

I've never been more
sure

Ace of Wands (Upright)

If I start walking
now

I can at
least say I
tried

Ace of Wands (Reversed)

As you told me
your plan
I couldn't
stop looking at
your
smile

to be loved
and

anticipated

Two of Wands (Upright)

Yes actually

you can keep
moving

how can you be still the
wind
is calling
for you

Two of Wands (Reversed)

How can I doubt
myself

I have never
steered
myself wrong

I am
unfamiliar with
the concept of
failure

Each experience is a
lesson learned

Three of Wands (Upright)

I would think the further I go
the closer I'd get

I feel like I'm in a
hamster wheel

the scene seems to
change
or
just shift I'm not
sure

I've been running for hours
without knowing
what for

Three of Wands (Reversed)

The walls are secure
you can
drop your shoulders

let your body
sink

the silence is
less heavy than you
seem to think

Four of Wands (Upright)

How far will the runners
from a strawberry go
before they
give up

they seem to
not notice
they're in the wrong
spot

Four of Wands (Reversed)

Why are you
yelling

I whisper

we are on
the same
team

Five of Wands (Upright)

I'm certain

even more so as
the paths split

I'm glad to have
had this opportunity

there are splinters
in my hand
but it was worth

every

bit

Five of Wands (Reversed)

The birds and
the breeze and
everything that might
fall in between

I hear your name
in everything around

I hope you hear it too
they're all cheering
for you

(me too)

Six of Wands (upright)

I didn't hear
the clapping

I spent the
whole time wishing
it would be over

now I'm
slipping
my legs won't
hold my weight anymore

I'm
falling but
I can't find the ground
and they've all left

I was going for
confident

Six of Wands (Reversed)

Why would I put
my shield down

I see what's
behind
your
back

Seven of Wands (upright)

You can talk
all you want just

stay where
I can see

I'd hate to have to
push you down
but I have
learned

to

strike

much more

than a chord

Seven of Wands (Reversed)

Together
on top of a
dandelion seed

dodging raindrops
like missiles

not sure
where they're going
but it's quick and

maybe

closer
to where they'd
like
to be

Eight of Wands (Upright)

You wanted it quick

you hoped for it fast

Why are you crying?

A thousand miles per hour
breezes flashing past

Seriously, stop crying.

lace up your shoes

take a deep breath

it won't slow down
just because you're scared

remember why you started to care

Eight of Wands (Reversed)

Eyes

at every waking moment

they say be who you were
when no one is looking

I wouldn't know
where to
begin

Nine of Wands (upright)

I heard a guy got
shot way more times
and
he is still talking
shit like
all the time

I wasn't expecting
real bullets

I
am not sure if

I am going to
survive

Nine of Wands (Reversed)

They mean it as a
compliment

they think
telling me

I'm strong

makes it okay
to carry this
alone

I already know

can I stop
proving it

Ten of Wands (upright)

No
I didn't ask to shift the
weight

didn't think you'd need to be
told

I've learned what I can
carry
and it's more than one should
hold

Ten of Wands (Reversed)

I never understood
wanting to
feel like a
kid again

until I realized
I
could be

any kid

any time

any place

Page of Wands (upright)

My daydreams
could be
predictions

if only my body
respected

my opinion

Page of Wands (Reversed)

Her eyes carry
everything I could
ever want to know

if her gaze ran
across acres and
days
there's no telling
how far I would
go

just to be seen
smiling
in the periphery

Knight of Wands (upright)

He said

if I die you're
coming with me

I smiled

I don't
think he realizes

what this gift means

Knight of Wands (Reversed)

If you must
follow someone
let it be me

I don't try

I don’t want

I simply speak and
it’ll be

Queen of Wands (upright)

He doesn't know
where the
power came from
he just knows
he wants it back

what's owed is owed
you'd do well
to not react

Queen of Wands (Reversed)

It's okay if you're scared
just move out of my way

you can stand behind
but I have lots of things I
need to say

King of Wands (upright)

take a look at
what i've done
and then
consider where
you would be

call it cocky if you
want

i'd much rather be
myself when it is
time to go to sleep

King of Wands (Reversed)

They'll use me as a weapon

you can have me for your shield

the truth
in all its glory

can't help but
be revealed

Ace of Swords (upright)

I hate when
people say

Retrace your steps

If I could remember
I would not be
cutting my
hands on the wire
trying to get
back

Ace of Swords (Reversed)

Aren't you tired
of
balancing

no one but you
cares

just take a step back

I won't tell
if you don't

I can wait while you sit

you have to
get comfortable between
the spaces of
where no one wants to be
if you want to
grow

Two of Swords (upright)

I am not
worried
about my secrets

I am worried

for your sake

why you would
try to
hurt
me

Two of Swords (Reversed)

Knowing why
doesn't
make it
easier

knowing why
makes me
sick

I am Caesar
as he watches

Brutus' hand
fall

Three of Swords (upright)

I wish you
didn't make
me prove
that I can
survive

no, I can
stand
grow
rise

without you

Three of Swords (Reversed)

If I could fix it all
I think I'd finally
be able to put
my feet up

will you watch the
door

I think it will
still be in need of
fixing
after a little
nap

Four of Swords (Upright)

I am
so tired but if

I fall asleep

I might miss something

I didn't
really
need to see

Four of Swords (Reversed)

I have the trophy
I am the winner
When will
Who cares
I won that's what
I was supposed to do
I got the medal
I won
When will

Shut up, I won

I thought
if I won
it was supposed to

I got the trophy
I won
who cares
I am the winner

Five of Swords (Upright)

I'm sorry we
yearn for martyrs and
endurance

You have earned to
forget

You don't have to
forgive

anyone but

yourself

Five of Swords (Reversed)

The air feels much
lighter the further
we go

can you feel the
exact moment
it's too high

I hope this becomes
like remembering
a lost tooth

Six of Swords (upright)

I know
it seemed familiar

and that is why
you stayed

there is no shame in learning
you started the wrong way

Six of Swords (Reversed)

Weird,

I thought
we were
friends

Seven of Swords (upright)

I would give
anything for
them to understand

it isn't naivete
I know the rules
too

I always knew

the thing with
forgiveness

it's something I
can
choose

Seven of Swords (Reversed)

That is not my
voice I'm just telling
you what it said

I know it's
"only in my mind"
do you think
I am choosing to
listen

I can't hear anything else
even as I try to
trace the silver
it quickly
turns to black
am I imagining
the sulfur in the
air as well

Eight of Swords (upright)

I am starting to
hear
myself

clearly

I am impressed by
my
voice

is this why they
look at me
I hope soon
I can see
what they see

Eight of Swords (Reversed)

Dried sweat and crusted tears

I should probably shower

they keep telling me
it's in my mind
I wonder how that makes
it less real

perception is the truth
so I avoid
sincerity

it's easy

plus

they prefer it that way

Nine of Swords (Upright)

Let go you are
bleeding on my floor

Stop

who told you to
grab the blade
in the first
place

Nine of Swords (Reversed)

They say
what doesn't kill you
makes you
stronger

they never asked if I
wanted to be strong
but they gave it their
best shot

I wonder if I want to
keep this up

what am I even doing

I want to live but I don't want to
be strong

Ten of Swords (Upright)

I am
grateful
and annoyed
to be another saying

It gets better

Just hold on

I wish
I could tell
you exactly
how I know
although
I am really
not sure though if
better means
good

Ten of Swords (Reversed)

Wouldn't it be nice to find the
words

the right ones without
teaching
too hard for balance

softness
would be comforting

your truth is somewhere inside
the skin of a
lemon

Page of Swords (upright)

I wonder if
seeing you
through my eyes
would make you
act more or
less like

yourself

Page of Swords (Reversed)

Love someone
who can take
control and I can
just be a
girl

don't ask me
I'm just here for the
ride he knows where
to go
I can just
close my eyes

I don't want to speak

and he can go fast as
he'd like

Knight of Swords (upright)

I'll keep my eyes
shut
when the wind
blows
too strong

if I pretend I'm
not moving
it's not on me when
we fall

Knight of Swords (Reversed)

To see you is to see
everything
all at once

I would give everything to be
the magnet
in your compass

your eyes are the
only safe place I
ever visited

Queen of Swords (upright)

I will not
apologize

you watched
as I sharpened
my knife

if you are cut
it's because
you
stood too close

Queen of Swords (Reversed)

He has
moved past the
need for validation
quicker than I thought

he likes when
I agree but
I am worried
I can't reach
the bar he
is raising
for me

King of Swords (Upright)

Of course the
solar flares
come now

I just calibrated
my compass

King of Swords (Reversed)

Dropped pennies
at the crossroads
the seed is out and dry

now we wait for the rain to fall

and see the harvest will rise

Ace of Pentacles (Upright)

I bet if
I saved that
money in
9th grade
instead of
buying cookies
at lunch
I could
afford

anything

Ace of Pentacles (Reversed)

I'd like to be a
goby

at the bottom of
the Red Sea

I can't imagine anything
better

I'd never have to stop
moving

still

if I wanted to

there's a
home

Two of Pentacles (upright)

They are
not impressed

but you should be

try letting
one go

they're not
even
looking

Two of Pentacles (Reversed)

To hear
and
to be heard
at the same time

to have my fire
met with wood
instead of
rain

Three of Pentacles (upright)

I'm not really
tired
I just kind of

don't want to

I could if I did

unfortunately

I don't

it doesn't matter
just feeling
scattered

Three of Pentacles (Reversed)

I never learned to
juggle

I was afraid
to let go

have you ever
watched as they
add more

and more

and more

Four of Pentacles (Upright)

Slán go fóill

I was scared to be
left
behind

but I'm glad I
don't have to
watch you pay the
toll

Four of Pentacles (Reversed)

They've turned
resiliency into a
compliment

I am
not sure why they
see the ache but
turn away

then if you
make it out
that's all they
will say

Five of Pentacles (Upright)

I have seen
the terror in
your face just
considering
a change

I can't stay here
anymore

I tried to help you
stand up
but you tried to
pull me
lower
I wish you
loved me more than
your
role

Five of Pentacles (Reversed)

I don't care
I really don't

If my stomach is full
yours will be too

if I am empty
it is only
because I'd like
to be

there is so
much more
than anyone
needs

Six of Pentacles (upright)

She makes promises
easily
because she doesn't intend
to follow
through

why did you keep
giving
now she's glowing in
your light
and they didn't even
see
you

Six of Pentacles (Reversed)

When you can
start to see the
finish line

your heart picks up

you don't even
notice the sweat anymore

your breathing
gets lighter

you wonder why
you ever doubted
you love the effort
it's worth the time

Seven of Pentacles (upright)

I spend all my time
working
and nothing is ever
seen

I am tired of
being
hidden

Seven of Pentacles (Reversed)

The storm will
never

The storm will
never stop

The storm will
never stop me

The storm will
never stop me from

The storm will
never stop me from catching dinner

–a spider

Eight of Pentacles (Upright)

Have you considered

actually
trying

Eight of Pentacles (Reversed)

My pockets know
no limits
my heart is
bursting full

the road was long
so lonely
and winding

glad I
focused on the
seed long before
the crop

I'll take a moment to
remember
but I'm
focused on who's
here

Nine of Pentacles (upright)

I have begun
to rot

I'm just glad
it's starting

from inside

Nine of Pentacles (Reversed)

There is nothing
I am incapable of

My roots stretch further than
you could imagine

My children's children
have silver spoons
and eat breakfast
on fine china

Ten of Pentacles (upright)

I'm not sure it's
okay

I don't care if it's
normal

I don't
want the same

or less

for the ones that will
be coming next

Ten of Pentacles (Reversed)

There is much to
be said
of a person that
makes nothing of
something

and something more of
a lot less

there's no pride in
overworking
but why be humble

you've
persisted

Page of Pentacles (upright)

I thought I
tried

well

I knew I could have
tried harder

it's bitter but

I will

try
again

Page of Pentacles (Reversed)

I didn't watch
John Henry
sweat himself to a
heart attack
to now pretend my
life is
too hard

I will yield my
hammer

I am
no machine

I am
not easily
broken

We
are not
easily broken

Knight of Pentacles (upright)

The concept of needing
to be reminded to
have integrity was
alien to me

but then I considered
I would rather die
than see my sons with
the vices that have
helped me to survive

I know I want them to be better

I know they want you to be bitter

Knight of Pentacles (Reversed)

I am soft and
there is
indeed strength in
staying so

and saying so

when the world around
you wants you
calloused and tough

I am not
fragile

I am and
I will
remain

soft

Queen of Pentacles (upright)

I still find myself hoping
she
was kinda like a
cuckoo bird

just left me somewhere
random

she
never learned to catch a
worm

she'd be a horrible bird
but
it would explain a lot

you know, they don't come back

anyway

Queen of Pentacles (Reversed)

If you'd stop pretending
it's normal to hoard

you would be
less impressed by
the ones pulling their
neighbors and even strangers
from sinking ground

even rats
know how to lend a
hand

King of Pentacles (upright)

I too have considered
the pros and cons
of really trying
in like
any way

I have grappled
with knowing there is
no way to ensure
anyone is going to be there

May I kindly suggest you
consider being
what you'd hoped for
and deserved
even just for yourself

Only temporary, the hell.

King of Pentacles (Reversed)

If you or anyone you know is in need of assistance finding their inner bad bitch (gender irrelevant) scan here:

Contact: TCS.LEGACY.WRITER@GMAIL.COM

www.ingramcontent.com/pod-product-compliance
Lightning Source LLC
LaVergne TN
LVHW090522110826
845146LV00003B/946

* 9 7 9 8 9 9 4 4 9 2 0 0 0 *